Savannah Cats and Kittens

Complete Owner's Guide
to Savannah Cat and Kitten Care

Personality, temperament, breeding,
training, health, diet, life expectancy,
buying, cost, and more facts

By Taylor David

Savannah Cats and Kittens
Complete Owner's Guide
to Savannah Cat and Kitten Care
Personality, temperament, breeding,
training, health, diet, life expectancy,
buying, cost, and more facts

ISBN 978-1-927870-14-3

Author: Taylor David
Copyright © 2013 Windrunner Pets
Published in Canada

Printed in the USA

Foreword

If you've never heard of a Savannah Cat, don't be surprised. They are one of the newest cat breeds around, only recognized by The International Cat Association in 2012. If you get online and search for a Savannah and think, "That looks like a miniature cheetah!" you won't be alone in the reaction.

The wild cat used to create this hybrid breed, however, is the African Serval Cat, a medium-sized cat weighing about 15-40 lbs. (7-18 kg). These slender, strong animals have bold black spots on a tawny background and generally feature two to four stripes running from the top of the head down over the neck.

They are widely distributed across Africa, and vary slightly in color and pattern by region. One thing, however, makes the Serval stand out. They are a gregarious and friendly species that, though solitary by nature, will live in close association with and interact with humans, even in their feral state.

This tendency toward a degree of voluntary domestication is part of what intrigued the first breeders to attempt a Serval / domestic cat cross. Even from the beginnings of the cat fancy with the first Crystal Palace Cat Show in London in 1871, however, there has been an interest in "wild" looking breeds.

Creating the hybrid known today as the Savannah was no easy project, however. The gestation period for a Serval pregnancy is 75 days, while that of a domestic cat is 65 days. Additionally, the two species have differing numbers of chromosomes.

In the first four generations of crosses, Savannah males are almost always sterile, further complicating the task of stabilizing the new breed. The fact that studbook tradition Savannahs exist today (four generations removed from their wild ancestors with three generations of Savannah-to-Savannah pairing in their pedigree) is testament to the dedication enthusiastic breeders brought to the creation of these spectacular cats.

From the F3 generation forward, the Savannah is a *domestic* cat. They are beautiful creatures, but they are not wild and they are not dangerous. They are, however, different. Savannahs don't just stand out for their good looks or for their amazing athletic abilities. They are highly intelligent, curious cats that are devoted, loyal, and loving companions.

A Savannah won't be in your lap (although he will hog the bed at night), but he will be in every facet of your life. If he isn't? He's miserable. Don't even consider getting a Savannah if you can't devote time and attention to be with your cat.

Also, be prepared for the price. Savannah cats are not cheap. Males cost $1,200-$9,000 USD / £784.68-£5,885.12 UK / $1,233-$9250 CAD and females run $1,200-$3,800 USD / £784.68-£2,484.83 UK / $1,233-$3906 CAD. (These are actually conservative estimates for SBT Savannahs.)

Foreword

But for those people for whom a Savannah is the right cat?
No amount of money is too much to pay for the
companionship and pure joy these remarkable animals will
bring into your life.

Acknowledgements

I would like to thank my two children for inspiring me to write this book. As an owner of a Savannah cat, I am so pleased with the temperament of this new breed, as well as its exotic look. After you read this book, you will have no doubt why they are worth such a pretty penny!

I'd also like to extend my thanks to my spouse who supports me in my every endeavor and who was the person who convinced me that our family should adopt another cat - a Savannah cat! Our children are loving this gentle hybrid cat that thinks it is a dog!

Table of Contents

Chapter 1 - Introduction to the Savannah Breed

The Savannah cat is one of the newest cat breeds, only gaining acceptance by The International Cat Club in 2012. Based on domestic pairings with African Serval Cats, these handsome hybrids with their exceptional personalities have taken the cat world by storm.

Many myths abound about their nature, habits, and capabilities, but one thing is certain. The Savannah is not a cat to be ignored — literally and figuratively. It is gaining popularity fast, and is well on the way to becoming one of the most popular of all companion breeds.

Savannahs are not typical cats, however, and they place unusual demands on their humans in terms of companionship and interaction. They are elegant, fascinating creatures, and if you decide you are the right fit for one of these exceptional felines, you will be gaining a devoted and loyal friend who will surpass your expectations from the moment he walks into your life.

Breed Development and History

The development of the Savannah breed began in the early 1980s when Judee Frank, who owned an African Serval, crossed it with a domestic cat. Her goal was simply to produce a companion for her wild pet. The result of the pairing was a female kitten named Savannah, who later had a litter of F2 kittens.

Frank did not pursue developing the breed, but she did sell one of Savannah's kittens to Patrick Kelly who began researching what would be needed to gain recognition for the intriguing new line of "wild" looking cats.

(Kelly continues to maintain the website SavannahCat.com, which is considered the leading online source for information about the breed.)

After failing to get a number of breeders interested in the Savannah project, Kelly approached Joyce Sroufe, who is now credited as the founder of the breed for her diligent faith and perseverance.

Her extensive knowledge of cat breeding allowed Sroufe to successfully produce a Savannah litter in 1994, and she is also recognized for producing the first fertile Savannah males. Since that time, Sroufe's cats have become the foundation of other breeding programs that she has actively mentored.

In 1996, Sroufe and Kelly presented the first breed standard for the Savannah to The International Cat Club. Unfortunately, the organization had a moratorium against new hybrid breeds in place at the time and the standard was rejected.

In 1997, however, Sroufe attended a cat show sponsored by TICA in Westchester, New York with a Savannah named Spanky. More than 5,000 people turned out to see Spanky after Sroufe gave an interview on her work with the hybrid cats. From the beginning, the Savannah was a show stealer, and it gained proponents quickly.

In 2001, TICA accepted the Savannah for showing, with F3 Savannahs becoming eligible for TICA new breed evaluation classes in 2002. These milestones were largely the work of Lorre Smith, the first TICA Savannah Breed Chairman, who was instrumental in getting the moratorium on hybrid breeds lifted.

As the Savannah has increasingly gained acceptance, these elegant cats with their exotic good looks and sweet personalities have become an instant hit at cat shows.

From the initial appearance of the breed, people clamored to get kittens even in the face of incredibly high prices. Even in the highly enthusiastic cat fancier community, the response to the Savannah has been overwhelming.

In 2012, TICA accepted the Savannah for Championship status. The breed continues to be actively refined today, and is rapidly becoming one of the favorite of all companion cats.

Similarity to Other "Wild" Breeds

The Savannah Cat is most often compared to the Egyptian Mau and the Bengal. The Mau is the oldest of all recorded cat breeds, and the only domestic cat with spots that occur naturally.

The Bengal was created by crossing domestic cats with the Asian Leopard Cat (ALC), while the Savannah breed is based on crosses with the African Serval Cat.

The Savannah breed was only recognized by The International Cat Association (TICA) in 2012, so there are still many F1 and F2 Savannah foundation cats with a high percentage of Serval blood.

These cats are distinct from the F3 and later Savannah Cats, including the fully domesticated stud book tradition (SBT) Savannahs that have three generations of Savannah-to-Savannah pairings in their pedigree. (This is a condition of TICA acceptance as a fully domesticated breed.)

Egyptian Mau

The Egyptian Mau is a moderately sized cat normally weighing 6-12 lbs. / 2.72-5.44 kg. The TICA accepted colors for the breed are silver, bronze, and smoke. They are very active cats with a higher than average intelligence.

Known for its sensitivity to its owner's moods, the Egyptian Mau is an affectionate animal that loves to be handled and cuddled.

They are energetic cats who will often play fetch, a game they punctuate with their graceful acrobatics. The breed is not, however, given to crazy bursts of activity, and they are only average talkers.

Because the Mau has a high need for attention, they do best for individuals who are home a great deal of the time or who have other animals.

The Mau does well in families and gets on with children of all ages who have been taught how to appropriately treat a companion animal with gentleness and respect.

Since the Mau tends to be shy around strangers, the breed does not do well to being re-homed. They are, however, very even tempered, and will simply hide if they are frightened. A quality pure bred Egyptian Mau sells for $500-$1000 USD / £325.83-£651-67 UK / $514.25 - $1,028.50 CAD

Bengal Cats

The Bengal is a medium to large cat typically weighing 8-16 lbs. / 3.62-7.25 kg. They are athletic and muscular with a decided daredevil streak.

Accepted background colorations for the breed include: buff, gold, rust, dark brown, silver, and snow. The most common nonstandard colorations seen for Bengals are blue, black, and charcoal.

A Bengal's rosettes range from rust and brown to pure black. The rosettes can be multi-colored, and a marbled pattern is also accepted as a breed standard. Some Bengals have the distinctive shimmer to their coat known as "glitter."

Although not a truly hypoallergenic breed, the Bengal sheds little and requires only minimal grooming.

People who are sensitive to the major feline allergen, the protein Fel d 1, show a lessened reaction to Bengals, so the cats can be tolerated successfully by some allergy sufferers.

Often described as "dog like," the Bengal is an intelligent, playful breed with a strong need to interact with their owners. They have a tendency to bond with one person in particular, but they are loving cats who will quickly become members of the family.

Easily leash trained, Bengals love to play fetch, and will have an opinion on everything you're doing. Although not as raucously vocal as a Siamese, Bengals make an astonishing array of vocalizations and use them all when they're trying to get their point across.

If left home alone, Bengals can get bored and get into trouble. They do well with respectful children and other pets, but should never be left alone with birds, fish, or hamsters. As a breed, they are sensitive to anesthesia and some vaccines. Expect to pay $500-$1200 USD / £325.83-£782 UK / $514.25 - @1,234.20 CAD.

Early Generation Savannahs

Savannahs in the F1 and F2 generation have a high percentage of African Serval blood. They can be large cats, but average about 18 lbs. / 8.16 kg. Physically they are tall, lanky and lean, appearing much larger than they actually are.

Accepted background hues include a warm gold to brown with silver spotted, black, and black smoke spotted coats present. Nonstandard coats include snow, charcoal, and black. The solid spots will be black or dark brown with some non-standard marbled and rosetted coats.

These cats are extremely active and motivated by energetic curiosity. They are highly intelligent and crave constant interaction with their owners, following their humans around, delivering powerful head butts, and happily walking on a leash.

F1 and F2 Savannahs are definitely not lap cats, and most do not like to be picked up. Their preference is to be near their humans, and they will sleep in bed with you, but they prefer involvement over most physical contact.

The climbing and jumping skills exhibited in these early generation Savannahs are phenomenal.

Absolutely nothing is out of reach for them, and once their curiosity has been sparked, they will not be satisfied until they have been able to complete their investigation.

Chapter 1 - Introduction to the Savannah Breed

It is quite common for an F1 or F2 Savannah to jump 8 to 9 feet (2.4 – 2.7 meters) from a sitting position. They can and will chew through anything and they are so clever they quickly learn to work levers and knobs.

These cats must be carefully placed with individuals or families that are home a great deal of the time and that understand how to deal with a hybrid cat this close to its wild antecedents. Some negative behaviors, like spraying in unaltered specimens, will still be present.

F1s and F2s exhibit extreme separation anxiety. Their need for human companionship is very high. Fortunately, they do get on well with both dogs and cats, but smaller pets, like fish, birds, or any kind of rodent will be perceived as prey.

Early generation Savannahs can be difficult to handle for vet visits and, if frightened, may visually and audibly warn you to back off. Under these circumstances, it's best to just let the cat settle down. They are not aggressive by nature, but are simply reacting out of fear and anxiety.

All Savannahs are highly sensitive to anesthesia, especially ketamine, and to some vaccines.

While you do not require the services of a wild animal veterinarian, it is imperative that the vet you do use understands the particular needs of the Savannah breed.

For males expect to pay:

F1
$12,000-$22,000
£7,846.83-£14,385.86
$12,342 - $22,627 CAD

F2
$9,000-$16,000
£5,885.12-£10,462.44
$9,256.50 - $16,456.00 CAD

For females:

F1
$12,000-$35,000
£7,846.83-£22,886.60
$12,342 - $35,997 CAD

F2
$9,000-$16,000
£5,885.12-£10,462.44
$9,256.50 - $16,456 CAD

A Note on Later Generation Savannahs

Note that all of the "negative" traits lessen and become more refined in later generation Savannah cats. A studbook tradition (SBT) Savannah has three Savannah-to-Savannah pairings in its pedigree and is specifically bred for positive traits.

The TICA show standard for this breed addresses behavior as a disqualification. "Temperament must be unchallenging; any sign of definite challenge shall disqualify.

The cat may exhibit fear, seek to flee, or generally complain aloud but may not threaten to harm. "

As this breed continues to evolve, the very best qualities of the Savannah will be those selected for organized breeding programs. There is no foundation for the concerns that a Savannah cat is "wild" or "dangerous" in any way.

Later Generation and SBT Savannah Cats

The farther removed a Savannah Cat becomes from is African Serval ancestors, the fewer "wild" characteristics it exhibits. It is generally accepted that F3 Savannahs forward make excellent pets.

An F3 Savannah is derived from crossing an F2 Savannah with a domestic cat. This means the F3 will have a African Serval Cat great-grandparent. In the next generation, the F4, the Serval will be the great-great-grandparent. SBT Savannahs are four full generations removed from the African Serval.

Size and Weight

In these later generations, the Savannah is a medium to large cat that normally settles in at a weight of around 16 lbs. / 7.25 kg, which is not significantly bigger than other large domestic cat breeds like the Maine Coon or the Norwegian Forest Cat.

Savannahs are quite tall, however. The current Guinness Book World Record holder for the tallest domestic cat is a Savannah named Savannah Islands Trouble. Though now deceased, Trouble was owned by Debby Maraspini. He stood 19 inches / 48.26 cm at the shoulder.

Coat and Grooming

The same golden and brown background colors with silver, black, and black smoke variations appear in all generations of the Savannah, as do the non-standard, snow, charcoal, and black coats. Solid spots are the standard with black to dark brown being preferred.

As a breed, the Savannah sheds very little and requires almost no maintenance. (Their fondness for getting in the shower with their humans is how most Savannah owners handle the issue of the occasional bath.)

No Savannah, regardless of its generation, is hypoallergenic, but many people who are sensitive to the protein Fel d 1 can tolerate being around these cats.

Activity Level and Personality

Even later generation Savannahs are extremely active, with a highly social, confident, and outgoing nature. Their energy seems almost boundless, as does their affection for their owners.

Motivated both by curiosity and intelligence, a Savannah wants to participate in your life complete with color commentary.

As the generations progress farther away from the foundation Serval, the cats become more hands on, but in general a Savannah prefers to be near you and observing rather than sitting in your lap or being held. All Savannahs, however, like to sleep with their humans.

Stunning athleticism is the hallmark of this breed. You will be absolutely astounded at your Savannah's ability to seemingly levitate from a sitting position, and as climbers, no other cat can touch their Ninja-like prowess. Expect to do some serious kitten proofing before you bring a Savannah cat home.

Due to the breed's tendency toward extreme separation anxiety — you do NOT want a bored Savannah getting creative — it's best for them to live with individuals and families who are home most of the time and have other animals.

Savannahs get along great with other cats and with dogs, but be careful with fish, birds, and rodents of any kind.

Like all companion animals, a Savannah cat will do best with children who have been taught how to be kind and appropriate.

A Savannah is not an aggressive cat, but no feline wants his ears or tail pulled. In the vast majority of cases it will be the child that is in need of correction rather than the cat.

Specific Health Concerns

All generations of this breed exhibit a potentially fatal sensitivity to anesthesia, especially ketamine, and to some vaccines.
(For a full discussion of Savannah cat health, see Chapter 4.)

While it is not necessary to engage the services of a special veterinarian, it is imperative that the vet with whom you work understands the Savannah breed and its unique sensitivities. Savannahs have an estimated life expectancy of 17 – 20 years.

For males, expect to pay:

F3
$3,500-$6,000
£2,288.66-£3,923.41
$3,599 - $6,171 CAD

F4
$1,200-$3,000
£784.68-£1,961.70
$1,234.20 - $3,085.50 CAD

F5
$1,200-$9,000
£784.68-£5,885.12
$1,234.20 - $9,256.50 CAD

SBT
$1,200-$9,000
£784.68-£5,885.12
$1,234.20 - $9,256.50 CAD

For Females:

F3
$3,500-$6,000
£2,288.66-£3,923.41
$3,599.00 - $6,171.00 CAD

F4
$1,200-$4,500
£784.68-£2,942.56
$1,234.20 - $4,628.25 CAD

F5
$1,200-$3,800
£784.68-£2,484.83
$1,234.20 - $3,908.30 CAD

SBT
$1,200-$3,800
£784.68-£2,484.83
$1,234.20 - $3,908.30 CAD

Note that costs vary widely by the quality of the cats. Most people will be buying "pet quality" Savannahs. These are animals that have been deemed inappropriate for showing or for use in breeding programs due to some perceived "flaw" that will likely be completely transparent to you.

The breeder will require that the animal be spayed or neutered, which is an effort to maintain and further the purity of breed as it evolves. This is actually a good stipulation, as pet quality animals sell for less money, and neutered individuals have fewer potential behavioral issues.

Chapter 2 – Buying a Savannah Cat

The Savannah Cat breed as we know it today is less than 20 years old and only received Championship status from The International Cat Association in 2012. Consequently, the breeder community is close knit and well connected.

One of the best resources to find a reputable breeder in your area is The International Savannah Cat Club, which maintains a website at: www.savannah-cat-club.com .

The site offers a full breeder directory and many useful resources to help you better understand this unique breed.

(Also note that we provide a list of Savannah breeders in the United States and in Europe in Appendix 2 at the back of this book.)

Locating and Working with a Savannah Breeder

When you have compiled a list of potential breeders, see if any are exhibiting their cats at shows in your area. Cat shows are an excellent way to see examples of the breeders Savannahs, and potentially to speak with the breeder.

Do not, however, expect to walk out with a cat, or to have a long, involved conversation with the breeder. Cat shows are highly hectic environments. Exhibitors have a limited amount of time to get to the ring when called, and handling cats is not allowed unless you are specifically asked to do so.

Think of visiting a cat show as "window shopping." If this is not an option, get on the phone and set up appointments to visit the catteries in which you are interested. You will want to meet the breeders, see their facilities, and meet some of their cats.

Never be offended at a cat show or at a cattery if you are asked to wash and sanitize your hands before handling a cat. Many feline diseases are highly contagious and can be passed from one animal to the next with nothing more than a nose tap.

You can be a carrier of disease as well. Breeders are safeguarding their animals when they ask you to sanitize your hands, and above all else, you want to work with a breeder who passionately cares about their cats.

Pay Attention to What You See at a Cattery

When you visit a cattery, you are evaluating the breeder as much as the animals. This is the place where your potential pet was born and has been socialized.

- Is the cattery clean and well maintained?
- Do the cats seem healthy?
- Are the cats reasonably confident even in the presence of strangers??
- How does the breeder talk about the cats?
- Does the breeder seem passionate about the animals?

Be wary of breeders that use phrases describing the Savannah as "wild" in any way. If anything, the breeder should downplay such qualities, emphasizing that the Savannah is a fully domesticated cat.

On the other hand, if you are interested in an early generation Savannah, an F1 or an F2, the breeder should emphasize just how close the cat is to its Serval Cat origins.

Note, however, that F1 and F2 Savannah Cats are only placed in carefully chosen homes. Typically F3 and later generations are made available as pets.

Finally, if you feel like the breeder is giving you the third degree, then you've likely found a really good cattery.

Breeders who love their animals are sending the kittens to new homes much like parents giving up children for adoption. They will want to know as much about you as possible and about how the cat will live in your home.

If the breeder isn't grilling you — even in a really NICE way — something isn't right!

How to tell if Your Savannah Kitten is Healthy

Healthy kittens have good muscle tone and clean, soft coats. Gently blow on the fur to part the hairs just enough to see the animal's skin. Make sure there's no flaking that might indicate dryness.

While you're at it, check right at the base of the ears and tail and under the "arm" pits. Make sure there are no tiny black specks that look like gravel. If it's present, you're seeing flea "dirt."

Fleas on a kitten are certainly not a deal breaker for an adoption. Catteries fight flea infestations all the time, especially in warm weather. You do, however, want to make sure you've gotten rid of the pesky little jumpers before you take the kitten into your house, especially if you have other pets already.

Make sure the kitten's eyes are alert, engaged, and bright. There should be no discharge either from the eyes or nose, and no sniffling or sneezing. Any of these things might indicate the presence of an upper respiratory infection (URI).

Specifically ask if any of the kittens in the litter have been sick. Feline diseases, especially URIs are highly contagious.

Finally, check the ears and make sure they are clean, with no internal debris.

Know the Signs of a Good Breeder

Recognize and watch for the signs of an exceptional cattery. Good breeders:

- Do not advertise in the want ads or put up flyers in pet stores or at flea markets.

- Are there for the cat for life. If you have to give the Savannah up for any reason, the first person you should be able to call is your breeder.

- Have a waiting list. You don't want a cattery that's just cranking out kittens. Being put on a waiting list means the breeding queens are well cared for and are not being stressed and harmed by excessive pregnancies.

- Require spaying and neutering for non-show animals. Expect to be asked to produce proof that the procedure was performed before you receive the cat's papers.

- Are happy to provide references of people who have adopted their cats in the past.

- Will explain to you how their kittens have been socialized.

- Are pleased to let you see the parents of the kittens and to give you a tour of the cattery.

- Have no qualms about discussing the pros and cons of owning a Savannah. You want a breeder who will tell you frankly that Savannah Cats are not for everyone, and who will back up that statement with honest insights and opinions.

- Address potential health concerns like the Savannah's sensitivity to anesthesia, especially ketamine.

- Love their cats to the point of choking up a bit even when they know the kitten is going to a superb home.

Although this is not a hard and fast statement, it is typically best to work with a breeder specializing in one breed only, especially with a hybrid like the Savannah. What you really want to avoid is falling into the trap of working with a kitten mill.

This is less a hazard with an expensive and specialized breed like the Savannah, but the more established these cats become, they will inevitably be produced by less than reputable breeders.

Do not consider it a negative if a breeder has their cattery adjacent to their home. With the Savannah in particular this is a must. These cats crave interaction with their humans. If one Savannah is demanding on its people, imagine the needs of a whole cattery full of them!

The Savannah Cat Breeders Code of Ethics

The code of ethics to which Savannah breeders adhere is a good guideline for what to expect in the adoption process. The section on "Registration and Sales or Transfer of Ownership" reads as follows:

Breeder Members of the Savannah Cat Club will:

1. Sell each kitten or adult with a written health guarantee, a three-generation pedigree, a record of immunizations, care and feeding instructions, and registration papers where applicable.

2. Inform the buyer of the characteristics of Savannah cats, and make available to the novice the benefit of his advice and experience.

3. Sell any kitten or adult having a known hereditary health defect or unsound temperament only with a Limited Registration and Spay/Neuter Contract.

If a kitten is sold as a companion animal, it may be sold one of two ways:

1. On a Limited Registration.

2. On a Spay/Neuter Contract whereby the breeder may withhold TICA registration papers until receipt of proof that the kitten has been altered.

The breeder shall remain responsible for the welfare of every cat he breeds, sells or places. This means making himself available to aid the new owner if and when the need presents itself.

If in the future the owner is not able to keep the cat, the owner should be instructed to contact the seller and the seller will have the responsibility either to take the cat back or find it a new home.

The breeder will not sell or dispose of any cat through pet shops, wholesalers, commercial dealers or paid agents. (**Source**: Savannah Cat Club, Inc. For the full text of the

Code of Ethics, see: http://www.savannahcatclub.com/docs/SVCC-code-of-ethics2.pdf)

Average Cost for a Savannah Cat

Although prices can vary widely by cattery, the following price ranges are typical for Savannah Cats:

Males:
F1
$12,000-$22,000
£7,846.83-£14,385.86
$12,342 - $22,627 CAD

F2

$9,000-$16,000
£5,885.12-£10,462.44
$9,256.50 - $16,456.00 CAD

F3
$3,500-$6,000
£2,288.66-£3,923.41
$3,599 - $6,171 CAD

F4
$1,200-$3,000
£784.68-£1,961.70
$1,234.20 - $3,085.50 CAD

F5
$1,200-$9,000
£784.68-£5,885.12
$1,234.20 - $9,256.50 CAD

SBT
$1,200-$9,000
£784.68-£5,885.12
$1,234.20 - $9,256.50 CAD

Females:
F1
$12,000-$35,000
£7,846.83-£22,886.60
$12,342 - $35,997 CAD

F2
$9,000-$16,000
£5,885.12-£10,462.44
$9,256.50 - $16,456 CAD

F3

$3,500-$6,000

£2,288.66-£3,923.41

$3,599.00 - $6,171.00 CAD

F4

$1,200-$4,500

£784.68-£2,942.56

$1,234.20 - $4,628.25 CAD

F5

$1,200-$3,800

£784.68-£2,484.83

$1,234.20 - $3,908.30 CAD

SBT

$1,200-$3,800

£784.68-£2,484.83

$1,234.20 - $3,908.30 CAD

Chapter 3 – Daily Care of Your Savannah

A Savannah is no more expensive than any other domestic cat to maintain as a companion. Their requirements for food and water are perfectly normal, though they are hard on toys and scratching posts.

The real thing you'll have to get used to is just how much your Savannah wants to be with you. They don't just like the companionship of their humans; they seek it. Your cat will follow you around the house, supervising and commenting on whatever you're doing.

He won't necessarily crawl up in your lap, but you'll get head-butted dozens of times an hour. Out of nowhere your Savannah will rocket by with a toy, or gracefully leap to the top of the bookcase to get a better view of something.

He'll sleep with you. Shower with you. Take walks with you on a leash. And he won't be happy when you go somewhere without him, bounding to meet you on your return, full of "news" about what he's been up to.

Leave a Savannah alone long enough for him to get bored and inventive, and he's liable to have been "up to" almost anything.

Clownish by nature, unbelievably devoted and loyal, and affectionate without being fawning, the Savannah is not your average cat. But once you've lived with a Savannah, you may never be able to settle for an "average" cat again.

Don't Just Kitten Proof, Savannah Proof

Think of your Savannah kitten as an incredibly agile toddler with an ability to take startlingly acrobatic leaps to investigate whatever strikes it's fancy.

He's a little daredevil, with no concept of his size in relation to the world. A supercharged bundle of energy on four paws, your Savannah will take the house by storm. It's your job to make sure the house doesn't fight back!

- Remove all small objects that could be choking hazards or could become blocked in the cat's digestive system if swallowed.

- Be especially vigilant about rubber bands and bits of string.

- Buy the most sturdy toys you can find and check them regularly for broken parts or bits that might be coming loose.

Step back and take a critical look at your house. If you were a small, adventuresome furry super hero what spaces would you try to get into? Block any place your Savannah can crawl into and get stuck.

You will also want to remove or secure:

- All toxic plants. (See Appendix 5 - Plants That Are Toxic to Cats for a list.)

- All human medications, both prescription and over-the-counter drugs. (Both Tylenol and aspirin can cause fatal reactions in cats.)

- All household cleaning agents.

- All insecticides or other chemicals present in the home.

- Heavy objects that could be tipped over.

- Electrical cables.

For anything like electrical cables that represent a chewing hazard, either run the cords through a PVC pipe to create a protective barrier, or spray them with Tabasco Sauce or Bitter Apple Spray.

Tie all hanging drapery pulls so they are out of the kitten's reach, and beware of rockers and lounge chairs. Kittens can get trapped inside and injured by the mechanical mechanisms.

As a standard rule of thumb, anything you would do to protect a small child in your home should be implemented to protect your Savannah kitten, including the use of child safety locks on cabinet doors.

Savannahs are very clever with their paws and can easily learn to turn door knobs and depress both levers and conventional latches.

Bringing a Savannah Kitten Home for the First Time

When kittens leave a cattery, their mother, and their litter mates they will need some time to adjust to their new surroundings in a quiet, stress-free space.

Keep you Savannah kitten in a separate room, like a bathroom or a spare bedroom, for at least two weeks.

Confine the Kitten to a Small Space

Start with a small space, where there's no way the kitten can get under anything and hide (or get stuck). Make sure your baby has its litter box, food and water bowls, bed, and some kitten-safe toys.

Use the Same Litter as the Cattery

Talk to the breeder about what the cat is used to for its litter box needs, and replicate everything exactly. Use the same kind of box and filler the cattery uses.

Cats that are stressed can easily go "off" their box and sometimes it's hard to get them back "on."

If you do decide to change the type of litter, do so gradually and only after a couple of weeks. If you want to use a different kind of box, don't take the old one away until the cat is using the newer model reliably.

Opening the Crate on Day One

On day one you will have transported your Savannah in a travel crate. Have all the accessories ready in the baby's "room." Put the crate down, open it, and let the kitten come out on its own.

As soon as it ventures out, gently show the kitten where the litter box is, actually placing the baby inside the box so it will feel the sand or gravel with its paws.

Have food and water out and ready, but let your baby Savannah explore and get comfortable on its own. Just be quiet and be with the kitten, talking softly and encouragingly.

Maintain a Two-Week Quarantine from Other Pets

After about a week, you can give the kitten a larger area of access, but keep the Savannah and any other pets separate for at least two weeks. This quarantine is for the safety of all concerned, to ensure that no viruses are transmitted in either direction.

Allow initial interactions with other pets to take place under closed doors. Cats communicate via scent and body language. They'll learn more about each other with sniffing and exploratory paw swipes than you might think.

Initial face-to-face introductions might include some hissing or bowed backs, but let the cats work it out. Above all, don't overreact and inject your own anxiety into the situation.

When the Two Weeks Are Up

When your Savannah kitten will come to you readily, you can allow it to have "run of the house" with supervision. It is a good idea to keep several small litter boxes throughout the house for the first couple of months.

Kittens are, after all, just babies. When they need to go they might not make it back to the box. The best way to avoid future litter box issues is to make sure they never get started! Keep the boxes clean, scooping litter daily.

It's also a good idea during the first two months to give your kitten some "time out" in its original room to encourage resting and regular use of a litter box in one location.

Baby Savannahs are dynamos that will wear themselves out completely if not encouraged (with a closed door) to settle down and get a nap!

Feeding Your Savannah Kitten

Discuss dietary choices with your breeder before bringing your Savannah kitten home and feed the cat whatever it has become accustomed to eating. Dietary changes with any breed should be gradual to avoid gastrointestinal problems

The goal it to meet your cat's optimum nutritional needs. Savannahs have a higher than usual need for taurine, which should be present in both their canned and dry food.

It's best to leave dry food out at all times for free feeding, with wet food given in the morning and evening, generally during the "crepuscular" or twilight hours.

Cats are not nocturnal. They are most active at dawn and dusk, so this is the perfect time to get them to eat well.

Since cats are obligate carnivores, the first listed ingredient in any high-quality cat food should be meat. As a general rule of thumb, the less expensive a commercial cat food product, the more plant filler it will contain.

Cats are not, nor can they be transformed into, vegetarians. They must have meat. Because of this fact, some owners choose to feed their Savannahs a raw diet.

This is not, however, just a matter of presenting the cat with some meat on a plate.

Considering the Raw Diet

Many Savannah breeders use the raw diet with their cats. It cannot be stressed strongly enough, however, that this is NOT a requirement of the breed itself, but a choice on the part of the breeder.

The following information is provided for the purposes of a well-rounded discussion of Savannah care. It is not a complete "how to" on feeding the raw diet.

Always discuss dietary requirements with both your breeder and your veterinarian.

Do not proceed with a raw feeding program until you fully understand your cat's nutritional needs and how the food is to be prepared with the correct equipment.

In theory, the raw diet is intended to give either a cat or a dog the food it would consume were it living in a natural state in the wild. For cats, that means what would be acquired from the fresh, whole carcass of its prey.
This diet is, however controversial, and many veterinarians are against the practice, citing the danger of salmonella infection, the potential failure to provide well- rounded nutrition, and the danger represented by bones in the food.

(Bone chards can cause a cat to choke, or they can seriously injure the throat, stomach, and intestines.)

When Feeding Raw Always Remember the Following

- Use only raw beef or chicken. Never give the cat pork or fish.

- Do not refrigerate raw food for a period longer than 2-3 days.

- Allow raw food to come up to room temperature on its own. Do not microwave.

- Maintain the highest standards of cleanliness for all receptacles and utensils, as well as for your work space.

- Invest in a quality grinder. It must be capable of safely reducing small bones.

Do Not Feed Raw Without Adequate Research

Never lose sight of the fact that an incorrectly prepared raw diet can be fatal to your cat. The diet includes bones, which can cause your Savannah to choke, or can tear at its throat and intestines. If you do not know what you are doing, do NOT feed any cat (or dog) a raw diet.

You must make these foods according to the standards laid out in set recipes utilizing the proper equipment and adhering to set rules of safety and hygienic preparation.

Again, your Savannah cat does NOT require a raw diet. They will do quite well on high-quality canned and dry foods with an occasional snack of cooked chicken or beef heart, kidney liver, or other meat.

Treats should be kept to a minimum with any breed, however. The point is to make sure the animal is getting the nutrition it requires.

Because Savannahs have a higher than usual need for taurine, commercial foods are likely your best bet, at least in the beginning.

If you are interested in the raw diet, it is not difficult to find the information online or to get feeding tips from established Savannah breeders.

Always Supply Fresh, Clean Water

Fortunately, Savannahs are good water drinkers, to the point that many will play in any source of water they can find. Many like to stick their faces under a running water tap as part of their self-grooming ritual.

Savannahs especially love water dishes with built-in circulating fountains. These units retail for about $30 US (£19.70 UK / $30.57 CAD). Yes, the cat will play in the water, and yes, you will have to clean it up, but your Savannah will be having so much fun, you'll be surprised at how little you mind!

Grooming Your Savannah

The short, dense coat of the Savannah requires little grooming. Brushing the cat with a wire brush once a week is more than sufficient to remove loose hair, but in truth, these cats shed very little.

It's quite common for a Savannah to just casually stroll in the shower with their human, which makes bathing the cat a snap. At that time, it's simple to clean your pet's ear flaps with a warm wash cloth. Otherwise? He's a pretty "wash and wear" kind of cat.

Finding Toys for Your Savannah

Savannahs are something well beyond hard on their toys. Don't think you can just give them some fuzzy little catnip mice or feathered birds. They'll have fun with them — for the five minutes they survive.

Unlike many cats, Savannahs are chewers, so in this regard, treat them like dogs. Go with toys suitable for small breeds of canine. You want things that are durable, and that have no parts that can come off and become choking hazards.

Savannahs do like to chase and fetch, so anything you can throw will go over big. Even the sturdiest cat toys should be "with supervision only." Only leave a Savannah alone with a toy that is exceptionally tough and able to take the abuse your cat is going to dish out.

Handling Issues of Scratching

Declawing is NEVER the answer to scratching issues with any breed. It is a cruel and inhumane amputation of the first joint of the animal's toe.

When cats have appropriate scratching furniture of their own — pieces that are large enough and engaging enough to attract their attention — they will use them.

If your cat shows an interest in the sofa, just spritz the animal with water and apply double-sided tape to the upholstery. Cats hate anything that is tacky to their paws. These scratching deterrents cost $8-$10 US / £5.25-$6.56 UK / $8.15 - $10.19 CAD.

If that fails to work, use herbal sprays like Pennyroyal or Orange Essence. Cats dislike both scents ($12-$15 US / £7.87-£9.84 UK / $12.23 - $15.29 CAD)

Clip your Savannah's claws once a month. If you start this grooming practice when the animal is a kitten, and are careful to clip only the white part of the claw, never the "quick," your cat will not object to the routine.

The smaller, more traditional scratching poles, which are covered in carpet, generally sell for $20-$30 / £12.74-£19.11 UK / $20.39-$30.58 CAD.

More elaborate and complex kitty "gyms," which are the better choice for an active, inquisitive breed like the Savannah, will cost $100 US (£65 UK / $101.95 CAD) to $300 US (£196.96 UK / $305.85 CAD) or even more.

Chapter 4 – Savannah Cat Health

Due to the newness of the breed, Savannah cats are exceptionally hardy animals, a trait that will only grow stronger as breeders continue to selectively improve their bloodlines.

There are no known genetic illnesses associated with the breed at this time, and Savannah cats do not require healthcare over and above what any domestic cat needs.

Owners must be aware of the Savannah's extreme sensitivity to anesthesia containing ketamine.

Spaying and Neutering: Anesthesia Concerns

As a condition of your adoption of a Savannah, you will likely have agreed to have the animal spayed or neutered before it reaches 6-8 months of age. It is quite common for a breeder to withhold transfer of the cat's pedigree until proof of the procedure is supplied.

It is a source of some frustration among pet owners that prices at veterinary clinics can vary so widely. You do not need the services of a special veterinarian to spay or neuter your Savannah. Any qualified small animal vet can perform the procedure, and it is possible to have the surgeries done for as little as $50 US (£32.82 UK / $51.08 CAD).

However, these procedures will require the administration of anesthesia, which does represent a potential danger to your Savannah, therefore the skill and knowledge of the vet is more important than the price. If you have just paid several thousand dollars for a cat, it makes no sense to go to a cheap veterinarian. It is imperative that any vet with which you work understands the Savannah breed and is open to the information you will supply, like discussions about ketamine anesthesia.

The owner of any hybrid breed is often in a position of having to gently educate the vet, so be prepared in advance to have this discussion. Stand your ground. Ask specifically what kind of anesthetic will be used and do not agree to move forward with the surgery until you have independently verified that any drugs that will be administered are safe for use with a Savannah.

Because the Savannah breeder and owner community is still relatively small, there are many active discussion boards online. Other owners are a great source of helpful information, particularly about matters pertaining to healthcare. Some examples of active discussion communities include:

- Savannah Cat Chat at www.savannahcatchat.com
- Savannah Cat Pets at pets.groups.yahoo.com/groups/SavannahCatPets/
- The Savannah Sections of CatForum.com

In the best of all possible situations, the vet you choose to spay or neuter your cat will become the animal's "primary care physician." Most pet owners prefer to have long-term working relationships with their vets, so err on the side of caution early on and find a veterinary professional who is a good fit for both you and your pet.

Important Vaccination Considerations

Like all companion animals, Savannahs can benefit from the typical regimen of vaccinations for such conditions as distemper and rabies according to regularly accepted schedules of immunization and boosters with one critical distinction.

Savannahs must NEVER be given either the FELV (feline leukemia) or the FIP (feline infectious peritonitis) vaccine. Both vaccines have the OPPOSITE effect in Savannahs and may well cause the animals to contract the conditions rather than provide immunity against them.

Vaccinations in both cats and humans have been a source of some controversy in recent years, centering on the potential for tumors to develop at the site of administration. If you are concerned, discuss the matter of vaccinations in detail with both your breeder and your vet to make sure that you are fully informed before making a decision.

The use of vaccines in both cats and dogs has been instrumental in reducing the spread of many highly contagious diseases and should not be discounted out of hand.

Typically, the schedule of vaccines a Savannah can receive would include:

- The distemper combo* at six weeks with boosters ever 3-4 weeks until 16 months of age. Another booster is given a year later, and then additional boosters are scheduled every three years.

- Rabies inoculations according to local regulations with boosters on an annual basis.

* The distemper combo includes antibodies for panleukopenia (FPV or feline infectious enteritis), rhinotracheitis (FVR is an upper respiratory or pulmonary infection), and calicivirus (causes respiratory infections). It may also include protection from Chlamydophilia (causes conjunctivitis).

At minimum vaccinations per individual shot will cost $40 US (£26.26 UK / $40.86 CAD).

Make Preventative Care Part of Daily Life

No one will ever know your Savannah better than you do. By being an observant and attentive owner, you can provide your cat with daily preventive health care simply by being vigilant for any signs of illness and responding proactively.

Typical Warning Signs of Illness in Cats

Savannah are such interactive and ever-present cats, it's not difficult to observe one carefully on a daily basis to keep an eye on its overall manner and condition. Some things of which you will want to take particular notice include:

- Weight gain or loss. A Savannah is a trim, muscular, athletic cat. You should be able to feel his rib cage just under a healthy pad of fat, but you should not be able to see the bones, nor should you have to go looking for them! Maintaining your cat at a healthy weight for life avoids a whole host of potential health problems.

- Physical motions. Your Savannah should be an exceptional athlete. Some can easily jump 8-9 ft / 2.4-2.7 m from a sitting position, as well as exhibiting an almost uncanny ability to climb. Any diminishment in these abilities or a reluctance to run, jump, or climb should be immediately evaluated by a veterinarian. Even a sure-footed cat like a Savannah can inadvertently hurt itself.

- A dry, bleeding, or stained nose. Always check your cat's nose for any signs of discharge. The area around the nose should be clean and well groomed, and the nose itself should be moist.

- Alert and engaged eyes. Savannahs watch everything. Always checks your cat's eyes not just for the quality of their expression, but also to be certain the pupils are equal in size and perfectly centered. The eyes should be well lubricated, with no discoloration of the whites and few blood vessels showing. If discharge and staining is present around the eyes, have the cat checked for an upper respiratory infection or allergies.

- Smelly, debris filled ears. Since the Savannah requires little grooming, it's recommended that when your cat casually strolls in the shower with you, which he will do, take a warm washcloth and gently wipe out his ears. This is a good time to make sure that the ears are free of black or brown debris and that no yeasty smell is present, which could indicate an infestation of mites. If your cat flinches or is vocal about having its ears touched, a vet should examine the animal.

- Discolored gums or dirty teeth. Since cats must be anesthetized to have their teeth cleaned, it's best to get your cat dental cleaning toys. Savannahs are VERY hard on their toys and most breeders recommend buying the tougher items normally purchased for small dogs.

Many of these toys are intended to clean the animal's teeth, so they're perfect for your cat. The Savannah's teeth should be clean, with no discoloration of the gums. Even if you don't have the cat's teeth cleaned, get your cat accustomed to having its gums examined for lumps or bumps. All cats are prone to oral cancers, so dental monitoring is extremely important.

While it is not impossible to get a Savannah to allow you to brush its teeth, this is a breed that prefers to be near its humans rather than in their laps. On a whole, less restraint with Savannahs is best.

When your cat is young, you can try a dental care kit, which will include a tooth brush and tooth paste. Most vets agree that if you can just get the toothpaste in the cat's mouth without a huge fight, you're ahead of the game. (Use only feline specific toothpaste with your cat.)

Dental care kits can be purchased from your veterinarian or in a pet store for approximately $7-$10 US (£4.60-£6.56 UK / $7.15-$10.21 CAD).

As you pet and stroke the animal, pay attention to any growths or lumps. These should be examined immediately by a veterinarian.

Thankfully, dehydration is not a problem with Savannahs. If anything you may well wish your cat was not quite so fond of playing in water! Even with all the happy splashing, make sure your pet has a constant supply of clean, cool drinking water at all times.

Litter Box Issues

Many hybrid breeds, including the Savannah, can develop litter box issues if they do not receive consistent training as young cats. It is extremely important not to make any sudden changes in your cat's litter box arrangements. Your kitten will be litter box trained when you bring it home from the breeder, but the stress of coming to a new home can put the cat "off" its box.

Be certain to use exactly the same kind of litter with which the kitten was trained, and the same type of box. If your cat does have an accident, don't assume the animal is acting out. Often if a cat has a urinary infection and tries to go in the box, the animal will associate the pain of the infection with the location and try to find another, pain-free place to do its business.

Neutered males can be subject to bladder blockages, so do not take any unusual litter box behavior for granted or write it off as the cat being "bad."

A change in litter box habits could even signal the presence of a disease like diabetes. Have the cat evaluated, and above all, don't yell and make a fuss. Put out as many litter boxes as you have to, but never introduce more stress into the situation. That will backfire on you and the cat will be even less likely to use its box appropriately.

Chapter 5 – Understanding Savannah Breeding

Starting a breeding program with any kind of cat is no small undertaking, but with a truly unique hybrid like the Savannah, you absolutely have to consider the nature of the animals themselves.

One Savannah will demand every ounce of attention you have to give, following you around the house and wanting to weigh in on everything you're doing. They don't like to be left alone, and while they're not lap cats, they need and want attention.

Now, imagine a whole herd of these beauties on your heels, head bonking you, and deciding to levitate on top of the tallest piece of furniture in the room — without warning — just because they can.

Savannahs are high energy cats and they take a lot of work!

Before Deciding to Become a Breeder

First, there's a hard economic reality you have to confront. No matter how expensive Savannah kittens may be, you are not going to get rich breeding these cats.

Every time you do sell a kitten, you'll start thinking about which bill needs to be paid first. In a cattery, money often goes out faster than it comes in.

Good breeders own up to this fact and share with you the one and only reason you should ever think of joining their ranks — love of the breed.

Get to Know Other Breeders

Getting to know other breeders and really learning what it's like to live with multiple Savannahs and to cope with the ups and downs of breeding pure bred cats is absolutely essential.

These are people who love their cats enough to tell you candidly what lies ahead. They're not worried about you, they're worried about the Savannahs you're going to be raising in the future!

There are many ways you can make contact with a good cross section of breeders. For one thing, just ask the breeder from whom you bought your own Savannah to introduce you to others in the breeder community.

- Visit cat shows for the express purpose of seeing Savannah cats and collecting business cards from exhibitors. Do not, however, try to get into a long, involved conversation with a breeder at a show. They'll be on a tight schedule and more than a little preoccupied.

- Locate and join a local or regional breed club and join online discussion forums where Savannah breeders and enthusiasts are active.

(Always abide by the correct etiquette when visiting an online discussion board. There should be a specific area of the site where you can introduce yourself as a "newbie." Read a lot, say little in the beginning. Learn the rules of the community and the personalities of the most active participants. Remember, when you are expressing yourself in writing only, your tone and intent can be easily misunderstood.)

Confront the Difficult Questions

The one person with whom you need to be most honest is yourself.

- Can you devote the necessary time to meet the needs of multiple cats every day, including holidays, and give them what they need in terms of attention, affection, and care?

- Do you have the money to get everything you need to run a cattery and to support it regardless of the amount of revenue you are or are not generating from the cats themselves?

- Do you have the space, or can you create the space, necessary to really meet the physical and emotional needs of an active, social breed like the Savannah? Do you realize this could even entail remodeling your home or building a separate building on your property?

- Do the people in your life support your plan and do they truly understand the time and money you're about to dedicate to this project?

- Should you need help, can you afford to hire someone?

- What is your plan for the care of your Savannahs if you do have to be away for business or a personal emergency? (It is critical that you have such a plan in place and that your cats already know and are comfortable with the person or persons who will be looking after them in your absence.)

- Do you have the stamina to hand-rear kittens should one of your queens reject her litter? This is a 24-hour a day proposition and it can be absolutely exhausting.

- Can you take it when sickly kittens die?

- Can you really give away kittens you've loved from the day they were born to a new home?

For many people, that last question is the real deal breaker. You are going to love these cats and they are going to love you. If you can't face the prospect of giving up so much as one of them, you do not need to be a cat breeder.

Try to Talk Yourself Out of the Idea

Play devil's advocate — ruthlessly. Consider every reason NOT to breed cats and ask yourself if you're falling for any of the "myths" that can be associated with the idea of raising even one litter.

- If I don't let my cat have a litter of her own, she'll mourn.

Okay, first, if you have adopted a pet quality Savannah, as a condition of the adoption, the animal will have been spayed, so who wants the kittens, you or her?

- Female cats need to have at least one litter before they're spayed.

Spaying should occur before 6 – 8 months of age. In fact, there can be serious medical complications when cats give birth at too early an age. Again. Who wants these kittens? You or your cat?

- My children need to have the experience of seeing an animal grow to maturity.

That's fine. Exposing children to the cycle of life — especially children raised in the city — is a worthy goal. However, you do not need to do that with an entire litter of highly specialized cats like the Savannah, nor do you need to establish a full-blown cattery to impart those lessons.

Besides, have you considered just how miserable your children will be when you let them raise a litter of kittens and then announce those babies are going to go away to new homes?

Breeding Cats is Not a One-Time Project

Crocheting an afghan is a one-time project. Running a cattery full of intelligent, emotionally needy Savannahs is a way of life. You will be making an enormous monetary commitment as well as joining a community of professional cat breeders so dedicated they have a code of ethics. This is not something to be taken up lightly!

Only be working with an established breeder can you get a real sense of the financial commitment you're about to make. Even the price of breeding queens and studs is far from "set" with Savannahs due to the newness of the breed.

Definitely work out an estimated cost sheet, and specifically ask the breeders with whom you are talking about surprise expenses they've encountered in their work. Your list will certainly include things like:

- reference books and materials
- medical testing before visits to/from a stud
- routine veterinary care
- emergency veterinary care
- kittening pens
- cat furniture and toys
- travel crates
- provisions for segregated housing of intact cats

Always envision the best, but budget for the worst!

"Are You Saying Don't Breed Savannahs?"

No. I'm saying think carefully before you decide to become a cat breeder with any pedigreed cat, but especially with the Savannah because they require so much of you.

Now, the flip side of that how much these animals give. Savannahs are remarkable cats. There is simply no breed like them, and you will likely be spoiled for any other cat once you welcome one of these tall, spotted beauties into your life.

If you have lived with a Savannah already, done all your homework, have the money and the time, and the support of the people in your life, breeding and living with multiple Savannah cats will be the experience of a lifetime!

Afterword

The hardwork and dedication breeders invested in crossing domestic cats with the African Serval Cat has given the cat fancy one of its newest and most intriguing breeds, the Savannah.

"Wild" in appearance, but gentle in nature, these intelligent, affectionate animals have been an instant hit since Joyce Sroufe first showed one off at a TICA-sponsored event in Westchester, New York in 1997.

In the intervening 16 years, breeders, many mentored by Sroufe herself, ushered the Savannah breed to its acceptance for championship status by TICA in 2012.

Although there are many myths about the Savannah (to the point that this book includes an appendix on laws governing the ownership of hybrids), these are fully domesticated cats.

From the F3 generation forward, they make excellent pets. SBT (studbook tradition) Savannahs are four full generations removed from their "wild" ancestor and have at least three generations of Savannah-to-Savannah pairings in their pedigree.

It's important to remember, however, that the wild ancestor in question, the African Serval Cat, is actually not all that wild. A small, solitary cat widely distributed throughout Africa, they are still gregarious animals with a tendency to voluntarily interact with humans, in part out of their native and insatiable curiosity.

The mix of this intriguing wild creature with domestic cats has given us the Savannah, a cat like no other. Tall, lean, superbly athletic, and companionably affectionate, once a Savannah comes striding into your life, your whole definition of "cat" changes forever.

A Savannah isn't the sort of cat to complacently settle down in your lap. He'd much rather be running your life, but he will do so with open affection, devotion, and a rather quirky sense of humor. You'll get your cuddle time at night when your Savannah takes over his side of the bed and most of yours!

If you and your lifestyle fit this breed's need for time and attention, owning a Savannah is an incredibly rewarding experience.

Relevant Websites

A1 Savannahs
The Original Founder of the Savannah Cat Breed
www.a1savannahs.com/

Select Exotics
The longest standing breeder of the Savannah
www.savannahcatbreed.com/

Savannah Cat Breed Information and Breeder List
www.savannahcat.com/public/index.php

The Savannah Cat Club
www.savannah-cat-club.com/

TICA Breed Profile
www.tica.org/public/breeds/sv/intro.php

VetStreet: Savannah Breed Profile
www.vetstreet.com/cats/savannah

PetMD: Savannah Cats
www.petmd.com/cat/breeds/c_ct_savannah#.UfFnEWTOu
Xo

Cat Breeds Encyclopedia
www.cat-breeds-encyclopedia.com/Savannah-cat.html

Video: A Beautiful Relationship
www.youtube.com/watch?v=zuiKbnA3w0Q

Relevant Websites

Video: Serval cat - tame wildcat
www.youtube.com/watch?v=gNs4m4JMxqE

Video: Savannah Cat TV - Cats have fun with a box
www.youtube.com/watch?v=Qg4pqEvPx5s

Video: F1 Savannah vs. Serval Cat
www.youtube.com/watch?v=JATR2DzG7A0

Video: F1 vs F5 (Savannah cats play fighting)
www.youtube.com/watch?v=uEJ6MWf0sCk

Savannah Cat Rescue
www.facebook.com/pages/Savannah-Cat-
Rescue/126186890732678

Savannah Cat Rescue
svrescue.com/home/

Frequently Asked Questions

I've been researching both breeds. Why should I get a Savannah instead of a Bengal?

Although the Bengal is a better known breed, there are major differences in the two cats. The Bengal is a smaller, compact cat with large rosette spots. It was developed from the Asian Leopard Cat, which is a less sociable and shyer wild cat than the African Serval used to create the Savannah breed.

The Savannah is long, tall, and lean in build with over-sized ears. It has a sweet, outgoing personality and a distinctly dog-like way of interacting with its humans.

There are many myths about the Savannah because the breed was only recognized by the International Cat Association in 2012, however, the cats accepted as pure bred Savannahs are four generations removed from their wild ancestors and are completely domestic.

Both cats are beautiful breeds with that highly desirable "wild" appearance, and both are loyal to the point of being "needy." Neither breed enjoys being left alone for long periods of time.

The decision of adopting a Savannah over a Bengal should be based on experiences with both breeds. Visit catteries where both breeds are raised and learn as much as you can about the animals.

Any companion animal requires a serious commitment, so know exactly what you're getting into before proceeding — for your own good, and especially for that of the cat.

How much can I expect to spend on a Savannah cost?

The price of any pure bred cat depends on the quality of the individual specimen, and the Savannah breed is very new and still under development. Because of this, varying "filial" degrees of the breed are available. (See Appendix 3 for an explanation of filial degrees.) The filial degree represents the cat's genetic distance from its wild ancestor.

Average price ranges are:

Males:
F1
$12,000-$22,000
£7,846.83-£14,385.86
$12,342 - $22,627 CAD

F2
$9,000-$16,000
£5,885.12-£10,462.44
$9,256.50 - $16,456.00 CAD
F3
$3,500-$6,000
£2,288.66-£3,923.41
$3,599 - $6,171 CAD

F4
$1,200-$3,000
£784.68-£1,961.70
$1,234.20 - $3,085.50 CAD

F5

$1,200-$9,000

£784.68-£5,885.12

$1,234.20 - $9,256.50 CAD

SBT

$1,200-$9,000

£784.68-£5,885.12

$1,234.20 - $9,256.50 CAD

Females:

F1

$12,000-$35,000

£7,846.83-£22,886.60

$12,342 - $35,997 CAD

F2

$9,000-$16,000

£5,885.12-£10,462.44

$9,256.50 - $16,456 CAD

F3

$3,500-$6,000

£2,288.66-£3,923.41

$3,599.00 - $6,171.00 CAD

F4

$1,200-$4,500

£784.68-£2,942.56

$1,234.20 - $4,628.25 CAD

F5

$1,200-$3,800

£784.68-£2,484.83

$1,234.20 - $3,908.30 CAD

SBT
$1,200-$3,800
£784.68-£2,484.83
$1,234.20 - $3,908.30 CAD

What is the life span of the Savannah breed?

The African Serval Cat from which the Savannah breed was developed has a life span of approximately 20 years. Domestic cats, on average, live 15 years. Savannah cats fall on the higher end of this scale, with an estimated life span of 17-20 years.

How large will my Savannah be when it's fully grown?

Earlier generations of Savannah cats, especially F1-F3 males, can be 20 lbs. / 9 kg and higher. Some breeders do place size high on their list of goals, but finding an exceptionally large Savannah is a very expensive proposition. In reality, the Savannah only looks big because they are such tall cats. The average Savannah is no larger than the common house cat, at around 15 lbs. / 6.8 kg.

What is it, exactly, that makes the Savannah unique as a breed?

The Savannah cat has a personality that is confident and bold. They are highly interactive cats with an inquisitive, playful nature that makes them both outgoing and extremely affectionate.

They are born investigators, intent on energetically discovering the world around them and being a part of anything that's going on in the house, especially if it's something new and different.

Expect your Savannah to always be around, looking to play and head bonk. From time to time they give in to "zooming," racing around the house for no apparent reason but the joy of being what they are. (Be warned, they don't pay much attention to anything that might be in their way!)

They are fantastic jumpers and incredibly busy. Most people who live with a Savannah will attest to the fact that the breed has a sense of humor and will actively play the clown.

They're always glad to see their humans, greeting you with a happy chirp, a meow, or an excited fluffing of the hair on their backs and at the base of their tail.

Simply put, there is no other cat like a Savannah, which is one of the reasons you must be fully prepared to welcome one into your life. Living with a Savannah is an incredibly rewarding experience, but it's not for everyone.

I've heard that Savannah cats are wild and dangerous. Is that true?

Many people make the mistaken assumption that because the Savannah was developed from the African Serval it must have a wild or feral personality and display traits that are dominant and aggressive. That's the farthest thing from the truth because the African Serval itself can be domesticated and can live as a house pet.

Under those circumstances, Servals can still be difficult and unpredictable, because they do not have a long history of domestication, but that does not negate the fact that they are interactive and gregarious by nature. Additionally, the Serval does not regard humans as prey.

Even an F1 Savannah cat is a good house pet, but they are extremely high energy animals. It's really the F2 generation and later that do better as pets, for the simple reason that their humans can keep up with them!

How would you describe the temperament of a Savannah?

The Savannah is loving and outgoing, with a very quick learning curve. These cats are smart! They rapidly become family members and will follow you around the house when you come home, conversationally filling you in on what they've been doing and thinking.

When a Savannah is playing fetch, he's delightfully goofy, and don't be surprised if in the summer he's happy to be sprayed down with the water hose or makes a perfect mess with any unattended water he can find in the house.

Savannahs that are trained early are excellent on leashes. (Training should begin as early as six months and be a completely indoor activity until the cat is totally happy wearing his harness and walking with the lead.)

Savannahs are really expensive! Why?

Producing a foundation cat that is a cross between an African Serval and a domestic cat is difficult. Males born in the first four generations are typically sterile.

There are chromosomal differences in the two species, and in their gestation periods. Many pregnancies end in re-absorption, miscarriage, or premature birth, especially when the father is an African Serval.

Breeding programs are expensive and involve permits that vary by location. This raises the cost of early generation Savannahs, but as you get into later generations, the price falls into a more reasonable range for a pure bred hybrid cat.

An F5 male will cost about $1,200-$9,000 / £784.68-£5,885.12, / $1,234.20 - $9,256.50 CAD with a female selling for $1,200-$3,800 / £784.68-£2,484.83 / $1,234.20 - $3,908.30 CAD.

What do the "F" numbers mean?

The "F" refers to the cat's filial generation. (See Appendix 3 for a complete description.) Basically, the "F" numbers are a shorthand way to reference how far the cat is removed from its African Serval ancestor.

An F1, for instance, has a Serval father, while an F2 has a Serval grandfather.

I'm also seeing designations with other letters? What do they mean?

Well, that can get really confusing, but here's a simplistic answer. When you see a letter associated with an F designation, the letter indicates how far back an outcross appears in the pedigree of that cat.

An "A" cat has a parent that is a non-Savannah, so by definition all F1 Savannahs are actually F1As because the Serval is a non-Savannah parent.

A "B" cat has one or more grandparents that are non-Savannahs, but both of its parents are Savannahs, so that cat has one generation of Savannah-to-Savannah breeding in its pedigree.

When you see a Savannah listed as SBT, that stands for "stud book tradition." It means the cat will have three generations of Savannah-to-Savannah pairings in its pedigree and is thus considered to be a fully domestic cat according to the rules of The International Cat Association.

Describe a household in which a Savannah cat will do well.

The Savannah is a highly adaptable cat. They prefer children who are respectful and well behaved, and will do nicely with existing pets that have a sociable nature. These cats thrive on activity!

How will a Savannah do with small children and other pets?

Savannahs are high-energy domestic cats. They don't require special supervision or housing around small children or other pets.

Any cat is going to react poorly to being mishandled by a child who has not been taught how to respectfully interact with the animal. In all likelihood, it's the child who will need more supervision than the cat!

Savannahs get on very well with dogs, but if you keep fish or have pet rodents . . . well . . . let's just say the Savannah will see them as live toys until they aren't live any more.

As for other cats, Savannahs will get on perfectly well with other species, but there will likely be some hissing in the beginning and the Savannah will wind up being the dominant cat.

This is not unusual, however, and it's best to let the cats themselves sort it out with gentle supervision.

Cats of all breeds rely on an intricate vocabulary of scent and body language to communicate. They are all territorial animals.

Even a perfectly normal "alley" cat will become highly aggressive when a new cat is brought into the household. Introductions through closed doors that allow for a lot of sniffing and exploratory paw play are best.

Will my Savannah need any special care or diet?

Again, a Savannah is a fully domesticated cat that will do well on any high-quality feline diet.

Some cat owners use homemade food and even feed raw, but these are highly specialized ways to feed a cat and should not be undertaken without a complete understanding of the requirements of feline nutrition. This fact holds true across all breeds.

Savannahs do require a higher amount of taurine in their diet and they are extremely sensitive to sedatives, which should only be used when absolutely necessary.

Never allow a veterinarian to use the drug ketamine with your Savannah, as it can be fatal.

I thought the Savannah had to be fed a raw diet?

This is but one of many myths about these cats. There are many cat breeders — with a wide variety of breeds — that use the raw diet.

All cats are obligate carnivores. They have to have protein. But their nutritional needs are much more complex than that. A cat will actually get sick if it's fed dog food because the preparation does not contain the correct combination of nutrients.

If you are interested in feeding any cat of any breed a raw diet, you must learn how to do so properly and you must acquire the correct equipment for preparation.

The raw diet includes feeding bones, which must be ground to a safe consistency to avoid choking and puncture hazards.

The raw diet is not as simple as just throwing some meat down on a plate and letting kitty go for it. Feeding a cat in this manner requires a great deal from the animal's owner. Don't even attempt a raw diet until you have educated yourself thoroughly.

Does the Savannah Cat have a highly developed predatory sense?

This perception stems mainly from the decision by the government of Australia to ban Savannahs out of fear that they represented a threat to endangered koalas.

The decision was based on sensational material gleaned primarily from the Internet and did not involve the input of Savannah breeders or cat judges experienced with the breed.

Consequently, the "super predator" myth is another fabrication that has become attached to the Savannah breed. It is preposterous. The Savannah is high energy, but it's no more efficient than any other domestic cat when it comes to hunting.

Are Savannah cats in love with water?

The African Serval hunts frogs and small fish in creek beds, and therefore goes in and out of water easily. Most Savannahs are more comfortable with water than domestic cats, and may join their humans in the shower.

They seem to prefer to be sprayed, or to put their own faces under running taps to help with grooming, but they don't like being put in water to be bathed. Their tolerance of and interest in water will vary by individual.

Is the Savannah a hypoallergenic cat breed?

The idea that the Savannah is hypoallergenic is also a myth. The breed does not shed much, so people who are sensitive to Fel d 1 (the protein that causes allergic symptoms), tend to have a lesser reaction to them.

Will my Savannah Cat require a special veterinarian?

No. Any regular vet that treats cats will be able to care for your Savannah. You should, however, be certain that your vet is familiar with the breed and knows of the high sensitivity these cats have to sedatives and in particular to ketamine.

Savannah kittens are not made available for adoption until they have been fully vaccination and are litter trained, so your kitten will come with pre-existing medical records.

Should a Savannah be declawed?

Adoption agreements typically stipulate that this breed (and any other breed of cat) must not be declawed. The surgery is illegal in Europe and in many parts of the United States. It is a cruel mutilation that removes the last digit of the cat's feet, destroys its ability to defend itself, impairs mobility, and is in no way necessary.

If you are not prepared for life with a cat — any cat — which includes managing some degree of scratching with appropriate deterrent like herbal sprays (pennyroyal and orange essence, for instance) and adequate scratching equipment — then don't get a cat.

How long does it take for a Savannah to grow to its mature size?

Although the rate of growth varies by individual, most Savannahs have reached their full size by 1 to 2 years of age. Earlier generation cats will mature more slowly, taking as long as 3 years to reach their mature weight.

Should a Savannah be allowed outside?

Only take your Savannah Cat outside on a leash and never leave it unsupervised. These cats are superior jumpers and left to their own devices, can get out of any enclosure. Once outside, they are subject to all the dangers that cats face in our modern world, from aggressive dogs to automobiles.

Savannahs, however, due to their wild appearance, are even more susceptible to harm from bad humans who, mistaking the cat for a wild species, may shoot and kill your pet.

Also, do not lose sight of the fact that you are adopting a very expensive and valuable cat. This is a new breed, only recognized by The International Cat Association in 2012. It is not out of the realm of possibility that your Savannah could be stolen.

Expect for your adoption agreement with your breeder to include a stipulation that your Savannah be an indoor cat, only allowed outside when leashed. This is a standard and very wise practice.

Why do breeders recommend that Savannah cats be confined to one room for the first 2 weeks after adoption?

First, it's important that your Savannah bond with you first, not with other pets in the household. For the first two weeks, you should be the center of your Savannah's new world. This is the time the two of you will get to know one another, so plan to spend lots of time with the kitten, playing and just talking to the cat.

Any time a new animal of any species is brought into a household it should be separated from existing pets to make sure no illnesses are transferred.

Two weeks is sufficient time for any common illness to surface. This practice isn't just for the protection of the Savannah, but for all the animals in the household.

A slow introduction among companion animals reduces stress and is recommended.

Remember that your Savannah has just been separated from its mother and litter mates. Your new cat will feel more secure in a single room.

If other cats are present in the household, expect a lot of under the door sniffing and paw play.This is perfectly normal and should be encouraged. Don't worry about any hissing or vocalizations.

All cats are territorial. They recognize one another by scent. They don't need to see each other in the beginning, but when they do, there will be some bluster and brag. Let them work it out, and above all, don't overreact. The cats will pick up on your anxiety and that will upset the acclimation process.

Also, in the absence of stress, your Savannah kitten will maintain good litter box habits in its new environment and get comfortable with the sounds of your household.

Often kittens "lose" their litter box in new surroundings or become fearful of a given area of the house when they hear something they don't like and have not had time to interpret.

If they have to "go," and they can't find their box, they pick what they think is the next best thing. You want to make sure that your Savannah kitten — or any kitten — has a clear sense of where its box is located before you let the cat roam freely in your house.

As your Savannah gets more comfortable, you'll see clear indications that it's ready to have a better look around — probably with you in tow so it will continue to feel safe. Remember, you are dealing with a highly intelligent and curious species.

By helping the cat to adapt slowly and securely to its new home, the transition should be smooth and the bonding process highly successful. Learn to take your cues from the Savannah.

This species is very good at communicating and those first two weeks with lots of one-on-one time in a limited space will allow you both to learn how to talk to one another.

Do I need to make any special housing arrangements for my Savannah?

Savannahs are domestic cats, so no special housing is necessary. If you've ever brought a baby cat home, you know that kitten proofing the household is a must.

All kittens of any breed are little daredevil demons with fur. They have no sense of proportion when it comes to their tiny size and the magnitude of the stunts they will attempt. Multiply that tendency to the power of 10 with a Savannah!

Put away any breakables, tape down exposed cords, make sure there are no choking hazards, or items that can be tipped over. Just in general assume you're bringing a toddler in your house and take all the same precautions.

(Child locks on cabinet doors, especially those containing household chemicals are a very good idea.)

Savannah kittens have something of a tendency to be a little clumsy when their frolicking around the house at high speed. They grow out of it, but when they're babies, they can be miniature menaces. Just be prepared — for your sake and for that of the cat.

(To learn more about kitten proofing your household, please see Chapter 3 - Daily Care of the Savannah: Not Your Average Cat.)

Appendix 1 - TICA Savannah Breed Standard

(*Source*: http://www.tica.org/members/publications/standards/sv.pdf)

HEAD - 40 points
Shape - 6
Ears - 7
Eyes - 6
Chin - 4
Muzzle - 4
Profile - 4
Nose - 3
Neck - 6

BODY - 40 points
Torso - 8
Legs - 8
Feet - 3
Tail - 7
Boning - 7
Musculature - 7

COAT/COLOR/PATTERN - 20 points
Texture - 8
Pattern - 8
Color - 4

CATEGORY: Traditional.

DIVISIONS: Solid, Tabby and Silver/Smoke Division.

COLORS: Black, Brown (Black) Spotted Tabby, Black Silver Spotted Tabby and Black Smoke.

PERMISSIBLE OUTCROSSES: None

HEAD:

Shape: The face forms an equilateral triangle: the triangle is formed by the brow line over the eyes; and the sides follow down the jaw bone with a rounded finish at the muzzle. Above this triangle the forehead and ears form a rectangle from the brow line to the tops of the ears. The head is small in proportion to the body.

Ears: Ears are remarkably large and high on the head. They are wide with a deep base. They should be very upright and have rounded tops. The outside base of the ear should start no lower on the head than the height of the eyes, but may be set higher.

The inside base of the ears is set close at the top of the head; ideally, a vertical line can be drawn from the inner corner of the eye up to the inner base of the ear. Ear furnishings may be present; pronounced ocelli are desirable.

Eyes: Medium sized and set underneath a slightly hooded brow. The top of the eye resembles a boomerang set at the exact angle so that the corner of the eye slopes down the line of the nose.

The bottom half of the eye has an almond shape. The eyes are moderately deep set, low on the forehead, and at least one eye width apart. Tear stain markings are present along and between the eye and the nose. All eye colors are allowed and are independent of coat color.

Chin: From the frontal view the chin tapers to follow the triangle of the head. In profile, the nose is slightly protruding so that the angle from the nose to the chin slants back which may cause the chin to appear recessed

Muzzle: The muzzle is tapered with no break. It falls within the bottom portion of the facial triangle that runs from the brow to the point of the chin. Whisker pads are not pronounced.

Profile: The forehead is a straight to slightly convex curve from the top of the head to the ridge just above the eye where there is a slight change of direction and a straight to very-slight concave curve from that ridge to the tip of the nose.

In profile, the face also forms a triangle from the top of the eye to the tip of the nose, turning to follow the jaw line and back up to the eye.

Nose: Viewing from the front, the nose is wide across the top with low set nostrils. In profile, there is a slight downward turn at the end, giving a rounded appearance. Nose leather is slightly convex and wraps up over the nose.

Neck: Long and lean.

BODY:

Torso: The torso is long, lean and well-muscled with a full deep rib cage, prominent shoulder blades, a slight, but not extreme, tuck-up and a rounded rump. The hip and thigh are full and long and somewhat heavy in proportion to the rest of the body.

Legs: Longer than average, well-muscled, without appearing heavy or overly delicate. Back legs are slightly longer than the front legs.

Feet: Oval, medium in size.

Tail: Medium to thick in width. Medium in length, ending between the hock and just above ground level when standing with preferred length just below the hock. Tail should taper slightly to a blunt end. Whippy tails are not desired.

Boning: Medium boning with density and strength.

Musculature: Firm, well-developed, yet smooth.

COAT:

Short to medium in length with good substance and a slightly coarse feel to it. Coarser guard hairs cover a softer undercoat; the spots have a notably softer texture than the guard hairs. The coat is not inordinately dense and lies relatively flat against the body.

COLORS:

Black, brown (black) spotted tabby, black silver spotted tabby, black smoke. No preference is given to ground color on the brown (black) spotted tabby. Bold, solid markings are preferred on all tabbies. In any variation the lips are black, and the tear duct lines are prominent. On the spotted Savannahs the nose leather can be pink to brick red surrounded by liner, solid black, or black with a pink to brick center stripe. In black Savannahs, the nose leather must be solid black. Paw pads in either color variation should be deep charcoal orbrownish black.

PATTERN: SPOTTED PATTERN ONLY.

The spotted Savannah pattern is made up of bold, solid dark-brown to black spots, which can be round, oval, or elongated. A series of parallel stripes, from the back of the head to just over the shoulder blades, fan out slightly over the back and the spotting pattern follows the line of the stripes from the shoulders continuing the length of the body.

Smaller spots will be found on the legs and feet as well as on the face. In the black Savannah ghost spotting may occur. A visible spotting pattern on the smoke Savannah is preferred. In all divisions, any visible pattern must be spotted.

TEMPERAMENT: The ideal Savannah is to be a confident, alert, curious and friendly cat.

GENERAL DESCRIPTION: The overall impression of the Savannah is a tall lean graceful cat with striking dark spots and other bold markings, on a background color of any shade of brown, silver, black or black smoke.

The Savannah cat is a domestic breed which closely resembles its ancestral source the African Serval, but is smaller in stature. Affectionate and outgoing, with exceptionally long neck, legs, and tall ears, as well as a medium length tail, the Savannah is both unusual and beautiful. The Savannah is alsoan exceptionally graceful, well-balanced cat with striking color and pattern.

ALLOWANCES: Females proportionately smaller than males

PENALIZE:

Rosettes. Spots that are any color other than dark brown to black. Any distinct locket on the neck, chest, abdomen or any other area not provided for in the standard. Vertically aligned spots or mackerel tabby type stripes. Cobby body. Small ears.

DISQUALIFY (DQ): Extra toes.

Temperament must be unchallenging; any sign of definite challenge shall disqualify.

The cat may exhibit fear, seek to flee, or generally complain aloud but may not threaten to harm. In accordance with Show Rules, ARTICLE SIXTEEN, the following shall be considered mandatory disqualifications: a cat that bites (216.9), a cat showing evidence of intent to deceive (216.10), adult whole male cats not having two descended testicles (216.11), cats with all or part of the tail missing , except as authorized by a Board approved standard(216.12.1), cats with more than five toes on each front foot and four toes on each back foot, unless proved the result of an injury or as authorized by a Board approved standard (216.12.2), visible or invisible tail faults if Board approved standard requires disqualification (216.12.4), crossed eyes if Board approved standard requires disqualification (216.12.5), total blindness (216.12.6), markedly smaller size, not in keeping with the breed (216.12.9), and depression of the sternum or unusually small diameter of the rib cage itself (216.12.11.1). See Show Rules, ARTICLE SIXTEEN for more comprehensive rules governing penalties and disqualifications.

Appendix 2 – Laws Affecting Savannah Cat Ownership

U.S.

Alaska
Hybrids are illegal to own unless grandfathered prior to Jan. 23, 2002, and are spayed/neutered, licensed with local officials, rabies vaccinated, registered with an approved registry, and microchipped.

(As per http://www.boards.adfg.state.ak.us/gameinfo/meetsum/2009-2010/prelim-actions-draft-sw10.pdf)

Alabama
No regulations at this time.

Arkansas
No provisions for hybrid cats.

Arizona
No provisions for hybrid cats.

California
The offspring of a restricted cat and domestic cat are not restricted.

(Section 671(c)(2)(K), Title 14, of the California Code of Regulations as per http://www.dfg.ca.gov/licensing/pdffiles/fg1518.pdf , page 8.)

Colorado
"While Colorado doesn't seem to have state-wide restrictions, Denver currently prohibits all generations of hybrid cat, but has a specific exclusion for later generation Bengals: 'this exception [that the cat is not a wild or dangerous animal] shall not apply to any animal that is the offspring (hybrid cross) of a domestic cat and any other species of cat unless the non-domestic cat ancestor was of the Bengal cat (Felis bengalensis) species and that all ancestors of the cat have lived in captivity for at least the preceding five (5) generations (F4) It is possible that this will eventually be revised to specifically name other breeds of hybrid origin once they have proven to be non-dangerous and wholly domestic."

(Source: www.messybeast.com/small-hybrids/ownership-hybrids-usa.htm)

Connecticut
All generations of Savannah are allowed per new bill SB1018 enacted in Jun 5, 2013.

District of Columbia
Savanna Cat Breed is allowed

Delaware
Permit required.

Florida
"Florida has an approach based on the appearance of the hybrids. 'Hybrids resulting from the cross between wildlife and domestic animal, which are substantially similar in

size, characteristics and behavior so as to be indistinguishable from the wild animal shall be regulated as wildlife at the higher and more restricted class of the wild parent.' F1, and some F2, hybrids would probably be regulated as wild animals, but the wording suggests that later generations are classed as domestic cats. While this sounds common-sense, it is comparable to the Dangerous Dogs Act in the UK where "experts" must determine from appearance alone whether a seized dog is a "pit bull type" and hence banned."

(Source: www.messybeast.com/small-hybrids/ownership-hybrids-usa.htm)

Georgia
Hybrids are illegal with special provision for Bengals

Hawaii
Savannah cats are prohibited.

Iowa
The Savannah must be the fourth or later filial generation of offspring with the first filial generation being the offspring of a domestic cat and a Serval, and each subsequent generation being the offspring of a domestic cat as of July 21, 2013.

Idaho
The statute suggests that F4 and later Savannahs are allowed

Illinois

In 2012 the Savannah breed was recognized for championship status by the International Cat Club which can only be achieved if the animal is considered fully domesticated. Such animals, in the state of Illinois, are allowed.

Indiana

Permit required for F1, no permit for F2 and later.

Kansas

Hybrids are allowed.

Kentucky

No regulations concerning hybrid cats.

Louisiana

The statute in Louisiana while specific to big cats like cougars and mountain lions is vague in regard to domestic cat hybrids like the Savannah. Presumption is that owners would do better with later generation cats.

Maine

No provisions for hybrid cats

Maryland

Later generations are allowed as they are more likely to be smaller. The requirement in Maryland is that the hybrid must be less than 30 lbs.

Massachusetts
In Massachusetts, F4 generation hybrids and lower are allowed. All generations are illegal in Boston.

Michigan
Savannahs are allowed.

Minnesota
SBT Savannahs are allowed. Hybrids are illegal in Minneapolis.

Mississippi
Requires special caging requirements and permits.

Missouri
Savannahs are allowed.

Montana
No restrictions on hybrid cats.

Nebraska
Hybrid cats are not allowed.

New Hampshire
Allows F4 and later generation hybrids.

New Jersey
No restrictions on hybrid cats.

New Mexico
No regulation concerning hybrids found.

Nevada

Later generation hybrids are allowed.

New York
F5 and later allowed in the state, but are illegal in New York City, Manhattan, Staten Island, The Bronx, Queens and Brooklyn.

North Carolina
Illegal in Wake County and New Haven County. Check the other counties as some have weight restrictions.

North Dakota
Permit Required

Ohio
Illegal to own hybrid cats.

Oklahoma
As long as a cat is not more than 50 lbs. exotic cats are permitted.

Oregon
Oregon Department of Fish and Wildlife does not regulate hybrids. There may be restrictions on the local level such as city or county ordinances.

Pennsylvania
The Pennsylvania Game Commission has determined that we have no prohibitions on the possession of the Savannah cat.

Rhode Island
Illegal to own a hybrid.

South Carolina
No provisions for hybrid cats found. Please check with state Fish and Game and local authorities prior to obtaining a hybrid cat.

South Dakota
License required.

Tennessee
No restriction on Savannah Cats

Texas
Texas counties that ban hybrids are: Austin, Bastrop, Bell, Bexar, Blanco, Burnet, Caldwell, Dallas, Denton, Hays, Lampassas, Lee, Milam, Montgomery, Odessa, Tarrant, Throckmorton, Travis, Williamson. Allows with special housing requirements: El Paso, Harris, Kaufman, Mason, Ward. You should check your county for specific requirements if your county is not listed above.

Utah
As Savannah Cats are recognized by The International Cat Association, they are allowed.

Virginia
Check your county for permit requirements.

Vermont
F4 and later are allowed.

Washington State

Illegal in Seattle. It is important to check with your state and local governments prior to acquiring a hybrid cat in this state.

Wisconsin

It is important to check with your state and local governments prior to acquiring a hybrid cat.

West Virginia

It is important to check with your state and local governments prior to acquiring a hybrid cat.

Wyoming

No regulations regarding feline hybrid can be found. However, it is important to check with your state and local governments prior to acquiring a hybrid cat.
No regulations regarding feline hybrid can be found. However, it is important to check with your state and local governments prior to acquiring a hybrid cat.

UK

Per Dangerous Wild Animals Act Section 5 – original wording - F1 Savannahs - license required.

F2 depending on percentage of African Serval blood you might need license. No license required for later breeds, however, it is best to purchase from a licensed breeder and get accurate information from there regarding licenses.

Australia– Illegal

Austria – F2 and later allowed

Canada
Alberta F1 to F3 illegal – F4 allowed
Ottawa – F1 illegal, may need permit for F2 – F4, F5 recognized as domestic cats
Saskatchewan – illegal

New Zealand – All generations banned.

Norway and Sweden – F1 – F4 banned, F5 and later are allowed.

Appendix 3 - Filial Degree Explained

The Savannah breed was created by crossing domestic cats with African Serval Cats. Breeds used to create the earliest Savannahs included:

- Oriental Shorthairs
- Egyptian Maus
- Serengetis
- Maine Coons
- Bengals
- Bengal Crosses
- Non-pedigreed domestic cats

The Savannah breed is still under development. It is common practice for later generation females to be bred back to African Serval Cats.

Savannah Males, on the other hand, are mated with Savannah females of all generations.

(In the first four generations, Savannah males are almost always infertile and adopted out to qualified homes.)

The first three generations to be produced from the mating of an African Serval Cat with a domestic cat are referred to as "Foundation Savannahs."

The word "filial" refers to the sequence of generations in a breeding program. Therefore, we have:

F1 - The first generation to result from crossing an African Serval Cat with a domestic cat. (Serval parent and domestic cat parent.)

F2 - The result of crossing an F1 Savannah with a domestic cat. (The cat has a Serval Cat grandparent.)

F3 - The result of crossing an F2 Savannah with a domestic cat. (The cat has a Serval Cat great-grandparent.)

F4 - The resulting of crossing an F3 Savannah with a domestic cat. (The cat has a Serval great-great-grandparent.)

No Savannah is fully recognized as belonging to the breed, however, until it has three generations of Savannah-to-Savannah mating in its pedigree.

An SBT Savannah (studbook tradition) must be removed four generations from its African Serval origins.

Through a dedicated core of breeders, the Savannah was fully recognized by The International Cat Association in 2012, having reached SBT status. Only an SBT Savannah is a pure bred, pedigreed, domestic cat eligible to compete in the show ring.

Appendix 4 - Savannah Cat Breeders

Austria

Akimba Savannah Cats
Elisabeth Haberhauer
Vienna
+43 1 920 46 63
members.chello.at/akimba

Canada

Shaghera Bengals & Savannahs
Michelle Boudreau
St. Hippolyte, Quebec
514.582.8798
www.f2savannahcat.com

NG Savannahs
Nathalie Gagnon
Quebec, Canada
418.878.1591
www.ngsavannahs.com

Lynx Creek Savannahs
Angie Panczak
Magrath, Alberta Canada
Tel: (403)758-3040
www.lynxcreeksavannah.com

WildStreak Savannahs
Teresa Adebahr

Surrey, B.C. Canada
Tel: (604) 591 6000
www.savannahs.webs.com/

CafeKitty
Randy & Christina Langelier
BC, Canada
Tel: 250.616.7113
www.facebook.com/The.Cafekitty

Catmopolitan
Carey Matthews
Victoria, BC Canada
Tel: (250) 294-2327
www.catmopolitan.ca/

Exotic Tails
Christine Avalon
Toronto & Aurora Ontario
Tel: (416) 265-4861
exotictails.ca/

Hilltop Pride
Carley Chapman
Ontario, Canada
Tel: (519) 623 2975
www.hilltoppride.com/

Spidersweb Savannah Cats
Anatole Cannon & June Rose
St. Catharines, Ontario, Canada
www.spiderswebsavannahs.com

Spots on the Lake
Lisa Jeffrey
Ontario Canada
Tel: 905-468-9204
www.savannahcat.ca

First Choice Savannah
Emma Savannah
Rive-Nord, QC
www.savannahf1cat.com

France

Chat-Savannah
Martin Francoise
Agde France
Tel: 21393
www.chat-savannah.com

ABC Savannahs
Patricia Frencken and Karin Koster
France and The Netherlands
Tel: 0031651785498
Tel: 0033233674075
www.abcsavannahcats.eu

Shaghera Benga et Savannah
Michelle Boudreau
Montreal, Quebec, Canada
Tel: (514) 582-8798
f2chatsavannah.com

Syminou Exotic Felines
Sybille Espinoza Parent
Valleyfield / Canada
Tel: (450) 373-5838
www.syminou.com/home.html

Umafelis Savannahs
Isabelle Merette
Quebec, Canada
Tel: (418) 659-5366
umafelis.com

Germany

Almasi-Savannahcats
Katrin Albertsmeyer
37339 Worbis Germany
Tel: 37339
www.savannahs-eichsfeld.de

Kiwanga
Margitta Graeve
+49 2763 1400
www.savannahcat.de

Savannahs of Malenga
Angelika Schaefer
www.savannahs-of-malenga.de

Shetani-Savannah Cats
Renate Remplein
Munich - Germany

Tel: (+49) 8208-90191
www.savannah-shetani.de

Holland
ABC Savannahs
Patricia Frencken and Karin Koster
France and The Netherlands
Tel: 0031651785498
Tel: 0033233674075
www.abcsavannahcats.eu

Ajabu Savannahs
Yvonne Brouwer
Ermelo, Holland
www.savannahcat.nl

Cattery Nevasirags
Ger en Grietje Klein
Winschoten (Netherlands)
www.nevasirags.nl

Italy

Urania Sphynx and Savannah Cattery
www.sphynxmania.com

Norway

No Cat Burglar
Mari Smith
Norway
www.nocatburglar.com

SavannahNorway
Camilla Hesby Johnsen
+47 917 24 990
www.savannah.no
Portugal

Bengalserver
Carlos Alberto Fernandes
Lisbon, Portugal
+351938404440
www.bengalserver.com

United Kingdom

Jacaranda Cats
Laura Buckley
Linton, Welcombe, Devon
www.jacarandacats.com/savannahs

Martin Thomas
Doncaster, South Yorkshire
martinthomas698@googlemail.com

Wicca Cats
Cynthia Hopper
Dover, Kent
44 (0) 1304 830904
www.wiccacats.co.uk

Bulgari Savannahs
Russell & Wendy Foskett
Hemel Hempstead, Hertfordshire, England

www.bulgaricats.co.uk

Russia

Savannah Spirit
Svetlana Berezina
Snezhinsk Russia
Tel: +79048039546
www.spiritsavannah.ru

USA Breeders

Alabama

Clawed Monet Cats
Donna Carlberg
Spanish Fort, AL
251.458.5480
www.facebook.com/carlbergdj

Dixie Dotz Savannahs
Scott Baumann
Trussville Alabama
Tel: (205) 281-4479
dixiedotz.com

Gotspots Savannahs
Pat & Jana Deleersnyder
Homewood, AL
205.249.7182
205.422.4565
frostjana@yahoo.com

Arizona

Amiri Exotics
Dawn Thomson
Douglas, AZ
Tel: 520-805-0889
www.amirisavannahs.com

Camelottaspots
Chris & Arden Morley
Arizona
Tel: 951-640-5293
www.exoticheritagecat.com

Thomwren Cattery
Marjorie Wren
Hereford, AZ
520.803.1559
www.thomwrencattery.com

California

African Veldt Savannahs
Elizabeth Villarreal
Los Angeles, CA
323.269.5595
www.africanveldtsavannahs.com

Designer Spots Cattery
Jennifer Malone
Ramona, CA
619.208.1561

www.designerspotscattery.com

Melissa Running
Pine Valley, CA
tedrunning@gmail.com
StoryTeller Savannahs
Nikki LaCrosse
Simi Valley, CA
www.storytellercats.com

Florida

Glitzycatz Savannahs
Susan Appenzeller
Tarpon Springs, FL
727.945.8803
savannahs@glitzycatz.com

Spotlight Savannahs
Melody Kyle
Pensacola, FL
850.377.7198
www.spotlightsavannahs.com

Illinois

CandC Savannahs
Callie Ingram
McLeansboro, IL
618.643.3930
www.candcsavannahs.com
CandC Savannahs

Carol Streit
Chicago, IL
312.446.3842
www.candcsavannahs.com

Summerwood Cattery, Inc.
Donna Lawver
Schaumburg, IL
708.721.0455
www.summerwoodsavannahs.com

Massachusetts

Tierboskat East Coast Savannahs
Bill & Dale Cuddy
Rowley, MA
978.948.7039
www.eastcoastsavannahs.com

New Jersey

Matthew Perlmutter
Mendham, NJ
essenwest@hotmail.com

New York

Savannahs of Manjaro
Lori Barnaba
315.200.2812
Jamesville, NY
www.savannahsofmanjaro.com

North Carolina

AJSavannahs
Adrianne
866.720.2951 toll free
www.AJSavannahs.com
Dream Weaver Catz
Shelby Sanford
Henderson, NC
252.438.2287
252.767.6679
www.dreamweavercatz.com

Oklahoma

A1 Savannahs
Martin & Kathrin Stucki
Ponca City, OK
918.671.7679
www.a1savannahs.com

Oregon

Angela Clements
Midland, OR
c000n@yahoo.com
Michael G. Gaither
Albany, OR
Grant06@aol.com

Lequoia Cats
Christina Goss
Lowell, OR
541.729.0684
www.lequoiacats.com

Pennsylvania

Kemple's Cats
Linda Kemple
Morrisville, PA
215.205.4728
www.kemplescats.com

Tennessee

Sadies Bengals & Savannahs
Clarksville, TN
Rise' D. Mikolajewski
931.552.3176
931.378.0949
www.sadiespets.com

Texas

Katznjamr
Jennifer Miller
Georgetown, TX
512.497.4298
www.katznjamr.com

UltimatExotics

Jacqueline A. Vulic
Magnolia, TX
713.918.9291
www.ultimatexotics.com

Utah

HP Savannahs
Ryan Wismar & Monique Sweeton
West Jordan, UT
801.918.8824
www.hpsavannahs.com

Snow Canyon Savannahs
Jannel Rockwell
St. George, UT
435.313.8591
www.snowcanyonsavannahs.com

Susan Bueno
West Valley, UT
suz@yahoo.com

Virginia

Spot On Savannahs
Georg & Lilli Anderson
Warrenton, VA
www.SpotOnSavannahs.com

Washington

Simply Savannah
Lisa Sauve
Tacoma, WA
253.847.1808
253.209.2043
www.simplysavannah.net

West Virginia

River Ridge Savannahs
Josie McInturff
Pipestem, WV
304.888.3108
www.riverridgesavannahs.com

Appendix 5 - Plants That Are Toxic to Cats

Source: The Cat Fancier's Association at www.cfa.org, http://www.cfa.org/CatCare/HouseholdHazards/ToxicPlants.aspx (Accessed July 2013).

While each of the plants on this list are toxic to cats, be especially careful of lilies. Savannahs are so curious and become so fixated on things they find fascinating, it's best not to have any of these plants in your house, and to keep your cat away from any that might be growing in your yard.

If your Savannah does eat any part of a poisonous plant, seek help from a veterinary professional immediately. Make sure the vet is aware of the fact that the Savannah is extremely sensitive to anesthesia, especially ketamine.

Almond (pits)
Aloe Vera
Alocasia
Amaryllis
Apple (seeds)
Apple Leaf Croton
Apricot (pits)
Arrowgrass
Asparagus Fern
Autumn Crocus
Avocado (fruit and pit)
Azalea Baby's Breath
Baneberry
Bayonet

Beargrass
Beech
Belladonna
Bird of Paradise
Bittersweet
Black-eyed Susan
Black Locust
Bleeding Heart
Bloodroot
Bluebonnet
Box
Boxwood
Branching Ivy
Buckeyes
Buddhist Pine
Burning Bush
Buttercup Cactus
Candelabra
Caladium
Calla Lily
Castor Bean
Ceriman
Charming Dieffenbachia
Cherry (pits, seeds, leaves)
Cherry Laurel
Chinaberry
Chinese Everegreen
Christmas Rose
Chrysanthemum
Cineria
Clematis
Cordatum

Coriaria
Cornflower
Corn Plant
Cornstalk Plant
Croton
Corydalis
Crocus, Autumn
Crown of Thorns
Cuban Laurel
Cutleaf Philodendron
Cycads
Cyclamen
Daffodil
Daphne
Datura
Deadly Nightshade
Death Camas
Devil's Ivy
Delphinium
Decentrea
Dieffenbachia
Dracaena Palm
Dragon Tree
Dumb Cane
Easter Lily
Eggplant
Elaine
Elderberry
Elephant Ear
Emerald Feather
English Ivy
Eucalyptus

Euonymus
Evergreen Ferns
Fiddle-leaf Fig
Florida Beauty
Flax
Four O'Clock
Foxglove
Fruit Salad Plant
Geranium
German Ivy
Giant Dumb Cane
Glacier Ivy
Golden Chain
Gold Dieffenbachia
Gold Dust Dracaena
Golden Glow
Golden Pothos
Gopher Purge
Hahn's Self-Branching Ivy
Heartland Philodendron
Hellebore
Hemlock, Poison
Hemlock, Water
Henbane
Holly
Horsebeans
Horsebrush
Hellebore
Horse Chestnuts
Hurricane Plant
Hyacinth
Hydrangea

Indian Rubber Plant
Indian Tobacco
Iris
Iris Ivy
Jack in the Pulpit
Janet Craig Dracaena
Japanese Show Lily
Java Beans
Jessamine
Jerusalem Cherry
Jimson Weed
Jonquil
Jungle Trumpets
Kalanchoe
Lacy Tree Philodendron
Lantana
Larkspur
Laurel
Lily
Lily Spider
Lily of the Valley
Locoweed
Lupine
Madagascar Dragon Tree
Marble Queen
Marigold
Marijuana
Mescal Bean
Mexican Breadfruit
Miniature Croton
Mistletoe
Mock Orange

Monkshood
Moonseed
Morning Glory
Mother-in-Law's Tongue
Morning Glory
Mountain Laurel
Mushrooms
Narcissus
Needlepoint Ivy
Nephytis
Nightshade Oleander
Onion
Oriental Lily
Peace Lily
Peach (pits and leaves)
Pencil Cactus
Peony
Periwinkle
Philodendron
Pimpernel
Plumosa Fern
Poinciana
Poinsettia (low toxicity)
Poison Hemlock
Poison Ivy
Poison Oak
Pokeweed
Poppy
Potato
Pothos
Precatory Bean
Primrose

Privet, Common
Red Emerald
Red Princess
Red-Margined Dracaena
Rhododendron
Rhubarb
Ribbon Plan
Rosemary Pea
Rubber Plant
Saddle Leaf Philodendron
Sago Palm
Satin Pathos
Schefflera
Scotch Broom
Silver Pothos
Skunk Cabbage
Snowdrops
Snow on the Mountain
Spotted Dumb Cane
Staggerweed
Star of Bethlehem
String of Pearls
Striped Dracaena
Sweetheart Ivy
Sweetpea
Swiss Cheese plant
Tansy Mustard
Taro Vine
Tiger Lily
Tobacco
Tomato Plant (green fruit, stem, leaves)
Tree Philodendron

Tropic Snow Dieffenbachia
Tulip
Tung Tree
Virginia Creeper
Water Hemlock
Weeping Fig
Wild Call
Wisteria Yews
English Yew
Western Yew
American Yew

Glossary

A

Ailurophile - A person who exhibits a deep love of cats.

Ailurophobe - A person who exhibits fear or hatred of cats.

Allergen - The protein Fel d 1 found in the saliva and sebaceous gland of cats is the allergen or irritant that causes adverse reactions in sensitive individuals.

Allergy - A reaction displayed by sensitive individuals to the Fel d 1, typically characterized by water eyes, sneezing, itching, and skin rashes.

Alter - The general term used to describe the procedure by which a companion animal is spayed or neutered rendering the individual incapable of fathering or giving birth to offspring.

B

Bloodline - The genetic line of descent for a pedigreed animal that establishes its lineage for purposes of registration and show.

Breed Standard - An agreed up set of optimum criteria for any breed of cat whereby individuals are evaluated for purposes of show and breeding.

Breed - Cats of a given lineage with similar physical characteristics that "breed true," meaning parents produce "like" offspring.

Breeder - A person who plans and operates a program of breeding or reproduction with a specific line of purebred cats for the purpose of show or sale and who works to both ensure and improve the genetic quality of said line.

Breeding - The pairing of male and female cats within a given breed to produce offspring.

Breeding Program - A program for the selective mating of cats to produce offspring that are superior examples of the breed.

Breed True - The ability of a male and female cat to produce offspring resembling themselves and that conform to the established standards of the breed.

C

Caterwaul - A feline vocalization that is shrill and discordant in nature.

Cat Fancy - A descriptive term for the large body of groups, clubs, associations, and individuals who are passionately involved in the welfare, breeding, and showing of various types of cats.

Cattery - A facility where cats are housed and often bred in an organized program.

Certified Pedigree - Registered verification of the lineage of a purebred cat affirmed by a recognized feline association.

Coat - The fur of a feline.

Crate - Small, secure containers designed to facilitate the temporary transport or confinement of domestic pets.

Crepuscular - Animals, like cats, that are most active in the twilight hours of dawn and dusk are said to be crepuscular. Cats are not, contrary to popular opinion, nocturnal.

Crossbred - An animal produced by the pairing of a male and female belonging to different breeds.

D

Dam - An alternate term for the female member of a breeding pair of cats. May also be referred to as the "queen."

Declawing - A controversial and inhumane procedure to remove the last digit of a feline's foot to render the animal incapable of scratching. The painful procedure also has the effect of depriving the cat of its natural abilities to defend itself.

Domesticated - Animals that by training and breeding live with and often work for human beings in a mutually beneficial and companionable relationship.

E

Exhibitor - Purebred cat owners who participate in organized cat shows.

F

Fel d 1 - A protein present in a cat's saliva and sebaceous glands responsible for causing an allergic reaction in sensitive humans.

Feline - Members of the family Felidae. There are seven species of "big" cats and 30 "small" cats.

Flehmening/Flehmen Reaction - A facial expression in cats that is often mistaken as a grimace or an expression of distaste. In reality, the cat is allowing air to move over two small openings in the roof of the mouth just behind the front teeth called Jacobsen's Organ. These specialized "second" nostrils give cats the ability to "taste" odor.

Free-Feed - The practice of leaving food, usually dry food or "kibble" out at all times for a cat to eat whenever it wishes.

G

Gene pool - Collective genetic information present in a population of organisms.

Genes - A DNA sequence occupying a specific area of a chromosome that determines the presence of given characteristics in an organism.

Genetic - Inherited tendencies, characteristics, conditions or traits present in an organism.

Genetics - The scientific study of heredity.

Genotype - The genetic makeup of an organism or a group of organisms.

Guard Hair - The outer layer of a cat's fur comprised of coarser, longer hairs.

H

Heat/Oestrus/Estrus - Heat is a female cat's period of sexual receptivity, characterized by yowling, rolling around on the floor, attempts to escape to the outdoors, and hyper-affection. Intact females go into heat every 2-3 weeks and remain in the condition for 3-16 days.

Hereditary - Genetically transmitted diseases, traits, characteristics, or conditions.

Housetraining - The process by which a cat is taught to urinate and defecate in a litter box so that it may live indoors cleanly.

Glossary

I

Immunization -A series of shots to inoculate an animal against an infectious disease. Also referred to as vaccination.

J

Jacobsen's Organ - Two small openings in the roof of a cat's mouth that allow the animal to "taste" a scent.

L

Litter - The number of offspring in a single birth. Generally 3-4 in cats, although 6-10 is not uncommon.

Litter Box - A container used by an indoor cat to urinate and defecate. Filled with commercial kitty "litter" or sand.

N

Neuter - The act of castrating a male cat.

Nictitating Membrane - A cat's third eyelid. A transparent, whitish inner membrane that closes to moisten and protect the eye.

O

Obligate Carnivore - Animals, like cats, that have evolved to and must consume an all-meat diet with no need to seek out plant-based foods.

P

Papers - Documented evidence of a cat's pedigree and registration.

Papillae - The tiny hook-like structures that line the tongue and gut of a cat.

Pedigree - The written record of a cat's genealogy going back three or more generations.

Q

Queen - A female cat capable of reproducing offspring.

Quick - The visible vein that runs into the base of a cat's claw that, if nicked during trimming, can be extremely painful and cause excessive bleeding.

R

Rabies - A highly infection viral disease typically fatal to warm-blooded animals. It attacks the central nervous system and is transmitted by the bite of an infected animal.

Registered Cat - A cat that is recognized by a feline association via proper documentation of its ancestry.

Righting Reflex - The ability of a falling cat to re-orient in midair in order to land on its feet in the vast majority of cases, but not under all circumstances.

S

Scratching Post - A structure covered in carpet or rope that allows a cat to sharpen and clean its claws inside the house without being destructive to furniture.

Secondary Coat - The fine hairs of a cat's undercoat.

Show - An organized exhibition for the judging of cats according to accepted breed standards with the concurrent awarding of signs of recognition, generally ribbons and/or trophies.

Sire - The male member of a parenting set of cats.

Spay - The surgery to remove a female cat's ovaries.

Spray - A behavior typically seen in male cats whereby the animal emits a stream of urine as a territorial marker.

T

Tapetum Lucidum - The highly reflective interior portion of a cat's eye that aids in night vision. This feature causes cats' eyes to glow in the dark and in flash photographs.

V

Vaccine - A weakened or dead preparation of a bacterium, virus, or other pathogen used to stimulate the production of antibodies for the purpose of creating immunity against the disease when injected.

Vibrissae - The coarse hairs commonly known as whiskers used to aid a cat with navigation and hunting.

W

Wean - Transitioning kittens from a diet comprised solely of their mother's milk to one made up of solid food. The process generally starts at 4-5 weeks of age and is completed by 8-12 weeks.

Whole - A cat of either gender that is intact, and has not been neutered or spayed.

Index

Printed in Great Britain
by Amazon